Chapter 1: Preparing for the Big Day

Chapter 2: Building Confidence

Chapter 3: Mastering the Basics

Chapter 4: Common Interview Questions

Chapter 5: Addressing Weaknesses and Failures

Chapter 6: Role-Specific Questions

Chapter 7: Behavioral Questions

Chapter 8: Situational and Hypothetical Questions

Chapter 9: Personality and Cultural Fit Questions

Chapter 10: Questions About Ambiguity

Chapter 11: Salary and Negotiation Questions

Chapter 12: Questions You Should Ask

Chapter 13: Following Up

Chapter 14: Evaluating Feedback

Chapter 15: 101 Questions and Answers

Part 1: The Foundations of Interview Success

Chapter 1: Preparing for the Big Day

1. Researching the Company and Role

Preparation begins with understanding the organization you're interviewing for.

- **Research the company**: Visit the company's website, explore its mission statement, and familiarize yourself with its history, products, services, and achievements.

- **Understand the role**: Study the job description to identify the skills, responsibilities, and expectations for the position. Take note of keywords that highlight critical skills or experiences required.
- **Explore industry trends**: Stay informed about recent developments in the industry, especially those relevant to the company's operations. This can demonstrate your enthusiasm and readiness to contribute.

2. Matching Your Skills to the Job Requirements

Once you understand the job's requirements, map them to your own skills and experiences.

- **Create a tailored skills list**: Identify specific examples from your past that align with the role's requirements.
- **Use the STAR method**: Prepare concise stories for interviews using the Situation, Task, Action, and Result framework.
- **Anticipate questions**: Review the job description and imagine questions the interviewer might ask based on it.

3. Organizing Your Portfolio and References

A well-organized portfolio can leave a lasting impression.

- **Update your resume**: Ensure your resume reflects the most relevant experiences and accomplishments. Tailor it to the role you're applying for.
- **Prepare references**: Choose references who can speak confidently about your skills and character. Inform them in advance and provide them with details about the position.
- **Create a portfolio**: Include samples of work (if applicable), certifications, or a list of major achievements to showcase your capabilities.

Job Interview Preparation with 101 Questions and Answers

Copyright © 2024 by John K. Zetak

All rights reserved. No part of this book may be reproduced, distributed, or transmitted in any form.

Disclaimer

The content of this book, *Job Interview Preparation Questions and Answers*, is intended for general informational purposes only and should not be considered professional advice. While every effort has been made to ensure the accuracy of the information provided, job interviews vary widely based on industry, company culture, and the personal preferences of interviewers. Therefore, the strategies, sample answers, and tips shared in this book should be adapted to fit individual circumstances and specific job roles.

This book does not guarantee employment or interview success. Readers are encouraged to conduct their own research, tailor responses to their unique experiences and qualifications, and seek additional professional guidance if needed. The authors and publisher disclaim any liability for decisions made based on the information presented in this book.

For legal or career-specific advice, consult a qualified professional.

Table of Contents

Chapter 2: Building Confidence

1. Understanding Common Interview Fears

It's natural to feel nervous about interviews, but understanding the source of anxiety can help you manage it.

- Fear of rejection: Focus on viewing interviews as a learning experience rather than a make-or-break event.
- Fear of the unknown: Preparation is key to reducing uncertainty.
- Fear of being judged: Remember, interviews are a two-way process. The company needs to impress you as much as you need to impress them.

2. Techniques to Reduce Anxiety and Stay Composed

- **Practice, practice, practice**: Rehearse your answers to common questions with a friend or in front of a mirror.
- **Relaxation techniques**: Use deep breathing exercises or visualization techniques to calm your nerves.
- **Positive affirmations**: Remind yourself of your strengths and past successes to build confidence.

3. Preparing Mentally and Emotionally

Confidence stems from mental and emotional readiness.

- **Visualize success**: Picture yourself handling the interview with ease and professionalism.
- **Create a pre-interview routine**: A consistent routine (e.g., a good night's sleep, a hearty breakfast, and some light exercise) can boost confidence.

- **Be kind to yourself**: Accept that perfection is not required. Focus on being authentic and prepared.

Chapter 3: Mastering the Basics
1. The Importance of First Impressions
First impressions matter and can set the tone for the rest of the interview.

- **Punctuality**: Arrive 10–15 minutes early. Being late can create a poor first impression.
- **Smile and greet warmly**: A genuine smile and firm handshake can establish a positive connection.
- **Be enthusiastic**: Show energy and interest from the outset.

2. Dress Codes and Body Language
- **Dress appropriately**: Research the company's culture to determine the appropriate dress code. When in doubt, err on the side of formality.
- **Maintain good posture**: Sit upright and avoid slouching.
- **Make eye contact**: It shows confidence and attentiveness.
- **Use open gestures**: Avoid crossing your arms or fidgeting excessively.

3. Etiquette for In-Person, Phone, and Virtual Interviews
- **In-person interviews**:
    - Bring multiple copies of your resume.
    - Respect everyone you meet, including receptionists and assistants.

- **Phone interviews**:
    - Find a quiet space.
    - Speak clearly and with energy, as your tone is the only tool to convey enthusiasm.
- **Virtual interviews**:
    - Test your technology beforehand (camera, microphone, and internet).
    - Ensure a clean, professional background and good lighting.

Part 1 equips you with the groundwork to succeed in any interview. From conducting thorough research to exuding confidence and mastering professional etiquette, these chapters ensure you'll start your preparation journey on the right foot.

Part 2: Essential Interview Questions

Chapter 4: Common Interview Questions

1. Question: Tell Me About Yourself

Answer Framework:

- Start with a brief overview of your professional background.
- Highlight 2–3 key achievements relevant to the role.
- Conclude by explaining how your experience aligns with the company's needs.

Example Answer:
"I have over five years of experience in digital marketing, specializing in SEO and content strategy. In my previous role, I increased organic traffic by 60% within a year, which significantly boosted lead generation. I'm passionate about leveraging data-driven strategies to drive business growth, which aligns perfectly with the goals of your organization."

2. Question: What Are Your Greatest Strengths?

Answer Framework:

- Focus on strengths directly relevant to the position.
- Provide specific examples to illustrate your skills.

Example Answer:
"My greatest strength is my ability to adapt quickly to new challenges. For instance, when my previous employer introduced a new software platform, I took the initiative to learn it thoroughly and trained the entire team within a month, ensuring a seamless transition."

3. Question: Why Do You Want to Work Here?

Answer Framework:

- Research the company's mission, culture, and recent achievements.
- Show how your skills and career goals align with the company's values.

Example Answer:
"I admire your commitment to innovation, especially the recent launch of your sustainability initiative. I'm excited about the

opportunity to contribute to a forward-thinking company that aligns with my passion for eco-friendly business practices."

Chapter 5: Addressing Weaknesses and Failures

1. Question: What Is Your Greatest Weakness?

Answer Framework:

- Be honest, but choose a weakness that doesn't undermine your ability to perform the job.
- Highlight the steps you've taken to improve.

Example Answer:
"I tend to focus too much on details, which can slow me down at times. However, I've started using time management tools to prioritize tasks and ensure I don't lose sight of deadlines."

2. Question: Tell Me About a Time You Failed

Answer Framework:

- Briefly describe the situation and the mistake you made.
- Emphasize what you learned and how you applied it to improve.

Example Answer:
"During a project rollout, I underestimated the time required for stakeholder approvals, which caused a delay. I learned to build buffer time into my project plans and improve my communication with stakeholders to avoid similar issues in the future."

Chapter 6: Role-Specific Questions

1. Tailored Questions for IT Roles

Question: How do you troubleshoot a critical system failure?
Answer Framework:

- Explain your step-by-step approach, emphasizing logical problem-solving and collaboration.

2. Tailored Questions for Marketing Roles

Question: How would you design a campaign for a new product?
Answer Framework:

- Discuss target audience research, creative strategy, and metrics to measure success.

3. Tailored Questions for Healthcare Roles

Question: How do you handle a difficult patient?
Answer Framework:

- Focus on empathy, active listening, and conflict resolution.

Part 2 Overview:
This section equips you with structured responses to common, challenging, and role-specific questions. By preparing thoughtful, tailored answers, you'll showcase your expertise, adaptability, and alignment with the company's goals.

Part 3: Tough and Tricky Questions

Chapter 7: Behavioral Questions

Behavioral questions require you to provide examples of past experiences to demonstrate how you handle certain situations. The STAR method (Situation, Task, Action, Result) is an effective way to structure your answers.

1. Question: Give an Example of How You Handled Conflict at Work

Answer Framework:

- **Situation**: Briefly describe the context of the conflict.
- **Task**: Explain your role and what you needed to accomplish.
- **Action**: Detail the steps you took to resolve the conflict.
- **Result**: Highlight the positive outcome.

Example Answer:
"In my previous role, a team member and I disagreed on the approach to a major project. I scheduled a meeting to understand their perspective and shared mine openly. We agreed on a middle ground that combined both ideas, which resulted in a successful project delivered ahead of schedule."

---

2. Question: Describe a Time When You Went Above and Beyond for a Project

Answer Framework:

- Highlight your willingness to exceed expectations.
- Provide a specific example and its impact on the team or organization.

Example Answer:
"During a product launch, I volunteered to take on additional

responsibilities when a team member fell ill. I managed their tasks alongside mine and worked overtime to ensure everything was completed. The launch was a success, and we exceeded our sales targets by 20% in the first week."

Chapter 8: Situational and Hypothetical Questions

Situational questions assess your problem-solving and critical-thinking skills by presenting hypothetical scenarios.

1. Question: How Would You Handle an Angry Customer?

Answer Framework:

- Acknowledge the customer's frustration.
- Demonstrate empathy and a focus on resolution.
- Explain steps you would take to resolve the issue.

Example Answer:
"I would remain calm and actively listen to the customer's concerns without interrupting. After understanding the issue, I would apologize sincerely and propose a solution to address their complaint. If needed, I would escalate the matter to ensure their satisfaction."

---

2. Question: Imagine You're Assigned a Task Outside Your Expertise. How Would You Approach It?

Answer Framework:

- Show your willingness to learn and collaborate.
- Highlight your problem-solving approach.

Example Answer:
"I would first research the task and gather as much information

as possible. If needed, I'd consult colleagues or supervisors with expertise in the area. By leveraging my resources and putting in the effort to learn, I'd ensure the task is completed successfully."

Chapter 9: Personality and Cultural Fit Questions

These questions help employers gauge whether you align with the company's culture and values.

1. Question: How Do You Handle Stress and Pressure?

Answer Framework:

- Describe your approach to staying composed under pressure.
- Provide an example of how you've successfully handled a high-stress situation.

Example Answer:
"I prioritize tasks and break them into manageable steps. For example, during a tight deadline for a major project, I created a detailed schedule and focused on completing one task at a time. This approach helped me deliver high-quality work on time."

---

2. Question: What Motivates You in a Job?

Answer Framework:

- Focus on intrinsic motivators such as growth, learning, or making an impact.
- Tie your motivation to the role you're applying for.

Example Answer:
"I'm motivated by opportunities to solve challenging problems and contribute to meaningful projects. For example, in my previous role, I led a team to streamline a process that saved the company significant resources, which was incredibly rewarding."

Chapter 10: Questions About Ambiguity

Ambiguous questions challenge you to clarify your career goals, priorities, and self-awareness.

1. Question: Where Do You See Yourself in 5 Years?

Answer Framework:

- Align your response with the company's goals.
- Demonstrate ambition while being realistic.

Example Answer:
"In five years, I see myself taking on greater responsibilities in [specific area], contributing to projects that drive innovation and growth for the company. I'm also eager to develop my leadership skills and mentor junior team members."

2. Question: Why Should We Hire You Over Other Candidates?

Answer Framework:

- Highlight your unique skills and experiences.
- Emphasize the value you bring to the role.

Example Answer:
"My combination of technical expertise and strong

interpersonal skills sets me apart. For instance, I've consistently delivered results in past roles, such as improving efficiency by 30% through process optimization, while fostering a collaborative team environment. I'm confident I can bring similar value here."

Chapter 11: Salary and Negotiation Questions

Salary questions can be tricky. Aim to show flexibility while advocating for your worth.

1. Question: What Are Your Salary Expectations?

Answer Framework:

- Research the market rate for similar roles.
- Provide a range and show willingness to negotiate.

Example Answer:
"Based on my research and the responsibilities of this role, I believe a salary in the range of [insert range] would be appropriate. I'm open to discussing this further to find a mutually beneficial agreement."

Part 3 Overview:
This section prepares you to handle the toughest questions with confidence and professionalism. By practicing structured responses, you'll demonstrate poise and adaptability, leaving a lasting impression on your interviewers.

Part 4: Asking the Right Questions

Asking thoughtful questions during an interview not only shows genuine interest in the role but also helps you assess whether the company is the right fit for you. This section provides examples of impactful questions to ask interviewers while highlighting questions to avoid.

Chapter 12: Questions You Should Ask

1. Questions About the Role

These questions demonstrate your eagerness to understand your responsibilities and the expectations for the role.

- **What does a typical day or week look like in this role?**
- **What are the most pressing priorities for this position in the first six months?**
- **How do you measure success for someone in this role?**

2. Questions About the Team and Leadership

These questions help you learn more about the work environment and team dynamics.

- **Can you tell me about the team I'll be working with?**
- **What is the management style of the person I'll be reporting to?**
- **How does the team collaborate on projects or handle challenges?**

3. Questions About the Company

Understanding the company's goals and culture is crucial to deciding if it aligns with your values and career goals.

- **What are the company's long-term goals or upcoming projects?**
- **How does the company support employee growth and development?**
- **What do you enjoy most about working here?**

4. Questions About Challenges and Opportunities

These questions show that you're already thinking about how you can contribute to the organization's success.

- **What challenges is the company or team currently facing, and how can this role help address them?**
- **What opportunities for innovation or improvement do you see for this role?**

5. Questions About Culture and Work-Life Balance

These questions provide insight into the company's values and how they treat employees.

- **How would you describe the company's culture?**
- **Does the company support remote or hybrid work options?**
- **What initiatives does the company have in place to promote work-life balance?**

Questions to Avoid

While it's important to ask questions, some can leave a negative impression or signal a lack of preparation. Avoid the following:

1. **Questions You Could Easily Research**
    - Example: *What does your company do?*
    - Instead, demonstrate that you've done your homework and ask more in-depth questions.
2. **Questions Focused Only on Salary or Perks**
    - Example: *How much vacation time do I get?*
    - While these are valid concerns, they're better discussed after receiving an offer.
3. **Overly Personal or Irrelevant Questions**
    - Example: *Do you usually work weekends?*
    - Stick to professional topics to maintain the right tone.
4. **Negative or Critical Questions**
    - Example: *Why did the last person leave this role?*
    - Instead, ask: *What qualities make someone successful in this position?*

How to Frame Your Questions

- Tailor your questions based on what you learned during the interview.
- Avoid asking questions that have already been answered unless you're seeking clarification.
- Be mindful of time—ask 2–3 well-thought-out questions instead of overwhelming the interviewer.

Part 4 Overview:
By asking thoughtful, strategic questions, you'll stand out as a candidate who is genuinely interested in contributing to the

company. Your questions also provide you with valuable insights to make an informed decision about the role and the organization.

Part 5: Post-Interview Success

A successful interview doesn't end when you walk out the door (or log off a virtual call). How you handle the post-interview phase can leave a lasting impression and increase your chances of securing the job. This section focuses on effective follow-ups, evaluating feedback, and preparing for future opportunities.

Chapter 13: Following Up

1. Writing a Professional Thank-You Email

A thank-you email is a simple but impactful gesture that shows appreciation for the opportunity and reiterates your interest in the role.

Guidelines for a Strong Thank-You Email:

- **Send it within 24 hours** of the interview.
- Address the interviewer(s) by name.
- Express gratitude for the opportunity to interview.
- Highlight a specific topic or moment from the interview to personalize the message.
- Reiterate your enthusiasm for the role and why you're a great fit.
- Keep it concise—4–5 sentences are sufficient.

Example Thank-You Email:

Subject: Thank You for the Opportunity

Dear [Interviewer's Name],

Thank you for taking the time to meet with me yesterday and share insights about [Company Name] and the [Role Name]. I truly appreciated learning more about [specific topic discussed], and it made me even more excited about the opportunity to contribute to [specific goal or value of the company].

Please don't hesitate to reach out if you need any additional information from my side. I look forward to the possibility of working with your team.

Best regards,
[Your Full Name]

2. Reiterating Your Interest

If you feel particularly passionate about the role, you can include a short follow-up email a week after the interview to restate your enthusiasm and inquire about next steps (if you haven't already heard back).

Chapter 14: Evaluating Feedback

1. Assessing Your Performance

Whether you receive an offer or not, every interview is a learning experience. Reflect on the following:

- What went well?
- Which questions were particularly challenging?

- Did you clearly communicate your strengths and fit for the role?

2. Handling Rejection Gracefully

If you don't get the job, maintain professionalism by sending a brief email thanking the interviewer for their time and asking for constructive feedback.

Example Rejection Follow-Up:

> Subject: Thank You for the Update
>
> Dear [Interviewer's Name],
>
> Thank you for letting me know about your decision regarding the [Role Name]. While I'm disappointed, I truly appreciated the opportunity to interview with [Company Name] and learn more about your team.
>
> If possible, I would greatly appreciate any feedback you could share regarding my application or interview performance, as I'm always looking to improve.
>
> Thank you again, and I hope our paths cross again in the future.
>
> Best regards,
> [Your Full Name]

3. Learning from Feedback

Take feedback constructively, even if it's critical. Use it to identify areas for improvement and refine your approach for future interviews.

Preparing for Your Next Interview

The end of one interview is the beginning of preparation for the next. Here's how to stay ready:

1. Keeping Your Skills Sharp

- Regularly update your resume and LinkedIn profile with new achievements.
- Stay informed about trends in your industry.
- Take online courses or attend workshops to enhance your skills.

2. Practicing Interview Techniques

- Conduct mock interviews with a mentor or friend.
- Review common and tough interview questions to refine your answers.
- Record yourself to evaluate your body language and tone of voice.

3. Expanding Your Network

- Stay connected with industry professionals through networking events or platforms like LinkedIn.
- Build relationships with recruiters and hiring managers.
- Join professional groups or communities related to your field.

Part 5 Overview:
The post-interview phase is an essential part of the hiring process. By following up professionally, learning from feedback, and continuously improving your skills, you'll be better prepared for future opportunities and increase your chances of success.

1. Tell me about yourself.

Sample Answer:
"I'm a marketing professional with over 5 years of experience specializing in digital campaigns. At my previous role, I increased online engagement by 40% through targeted social media strategies. I'm passionate about using data-driven insights to create impactful campaigns, and I'm excited about the opportunity to bring this expertise to your team."

---

2. What is your greatest weakness?

Sample Answer:
"One area I've been working on is public speaking. While I've always been comfortable with one-on-one discussions, presenting to larger audiences was a challenge for me. To improve, I enrolled in a public speaking course and have since delivered three successful presentations at company meetings."

---

3. Why should we hire you?

Sample Answer:
"I bring a unique combination of skills and experiences that align perfectly with this role. My background in project management and my ability to meet tight deadlines while maintaining quality would be valuable in this fast-paced environment. Additionally, my passion for innovation aligns with your company's mission."

4. Describe a time when you had to deal with conflict at work.

Sample Answer:

"In my previous role, I managed a team with diverse work styles. One time, two team members disagreed on how to approach a project. I facilitated a meeting where both shared their perspectives. By focusing on the project's objectives, we found a middle ground that leveraged their strengths, resulting in a successful outcome."

---

5. Where do you see yourself in 5 years?

Sample Answer:

"In 5 years, I hope to have grown within the company, taking on more responsibility and contributing to strategic projects. My goal is to continue developing my skills in [specific area] and take on leadership opportunities that drive team success."

---

6. How do you handle tight deadlines?

Sample Answer:

"I thrive under pressure and use organizational tools to stay on top of deadlines. For example, in a previous project, I prioritized tasks using project management software and communicated with the team to ensure we delivered on time. We not only met the deadline but exceeded client expectations."

---

7. Tell me about a time you failed.

Sample Answer:

"In my early career, I underestimated the time required for a client deliverable. The project was delayed, and I realized the importance of setting realistic timelines. Since then, I've developed better planning skills and now account for contingencies to ensure deadlines are met."

---

8. How do you prioritize your workload?

Sample Answer:
"I start by assessing tasks based on deadlines and impact. For instance, I use the Eisenhower Matrix to determine which tasks require immediate attention and which can be scheduled or delegated. This approach ensures I focus on what's most critical."

---

9. What motivates you?

Sample Answer:
"I'm motivated by solving challenges and seeing the results of my efforts. For example, in my last role, I spearheaded a cost-reduction initiative that saved the company 15%. The tangible impact of my work keeps me driven."

---

10. What are your salary expectations?

Sample Answer:
"Based on my research of industry standards and the responsibilities of this role, I believe a range of $X to $Y is appropriate. I'm open to discussing this further as I'm very excited about the opportunity to join your team."

11. Why did you stay unemployed for so long?

Sample Answer:

"During my time away from work, I focused on personal and professional growth. I completed a certification in [relevant field], worked on a freelance basis to maintain my skills, and took time to reassess my career goals. These experiences have given me clarity and prepared me for this opportunity."

---

12. Why are you leaving your current job?

Sample Answer:

"I'm looking for a new challenge where I can utilize my skills more effectively and contribute to a dynamic team. While I've gained a lot from my current role, I'm excited about the opportunity to grow further and take on new responsibilities."

---

13. Why do you want to work here?

Sample Answer:

"I admire your company's commitment to [specific value, e.g., innovation, sustainability], and I'm excited about the opportunity to contribute to [specific project or goal]. My skills in [specific skill] align well with the role, and I'm drawn to your company culture."

---

14. Can you explain the gap in your employment history?

Sample Answer:

"During that time, I focused on [reason, e.g., taking care of a family member, professional development, or personal projects]. I also used the time to [list productive activities, e.g., volunteer work, taking online courses], which allowed me to refine my skills and prepare for my next role."

15. Tell me about a time when you had to handle a difficult situation at work.

Sample Answer:
"In a previous role, a major client was unhappy due to a delay in project delivery. I immediately contacted them to understand their concerns, worked with my team to expedite the process, and provided regular updates. The client appreciated the communication and continued to work with us."

16. How do you handle criticism?

Sample Answer:
"I view constructive criticism as an opportunity to grow. For instance, in a performance review, I received feedback about improving my time management. I implemented productivity tools and saw significant improvements, which my manager acknowledged in the following review."

17. Why were you fired from your last job?

Sample Answer:
"My previous role wasn't the right fit for my skills and long-term career goals. However, I've taken the opportunity to reflect, develop my skills, and ensure that my next role aligns better with my strengths and values."

18. How do you handle stress and pressure?
Sample Answer:
"I stay calm under pressure by breaking tasks into smaller steps and prioritizing them. For example, during a tight deadline in my previous role, I delegated tasks to my team, set clear timelines, and ensured open communication, which helped us deliver on time."

---

19. What do you know about our company?
Sample Answer:
"I know your company is a leader in [specific industry/area] and has been recognized for [specific achievement]. I'm particularly impressed by your commitment to [specific value, e.g., innovation, customer satisfaction], and I'm excited about the opportunity to contribute to your mission."

---

20. What's your biggest professional accomplishment?
Sample Answer:
"In my last role, I spearheaded a project that improved operational efficiency by 25%, saving the company $50,000 annually. It was rewarding to see the positive impact of my work on the organization."

---

21. What makes you think you're better than other candidates for this role?
Sample Answer:
"I can't speak to the qualifications of other candidates, but I

can highlight what I bring to the table. My track record of [specific achievement], combined with my ability to adapt quickly and my passion for [specific field], makes me confident that I can contribute significantly to your team's success."

22. Why did you fail to achieve your goals in your last role?

Sample Answer:
"In one instance, I set an ambitious goal to increase sales by 50%, but we fell short, achieving a 35% increase. I learned the importance of balancing ambition with realistic planning and ensuring better team alignment. I've since improved my ability to set and achieve goals."

23. Why have you had so many jobs in a short period?

Sample Answer:
"I've had several roles because I've been exploring different industries and opportunities to find the best fit for my skills and career aspirations. Each role has taught me valuable lessons and helped me develop skills that I'm eager to bring to a long-term position like this one."

24. If you could change one thing about your past, what would it be?

Sample Answer:
"I would have started prioritizing mentorship earlier in my career. Although I learned a lot through trial and error, seeking advice from experienced professionals earlier would have

accelerated my growth. That's why I now make a point of learning from mentors and peers."

---

25. Why were you passed over for a promotion at your last job?

Sample Answer:
"At the time, the promotion required skills that I was still in the process of developing. Instead of dwelling on it, I sought opportunities to gain those skills, including [specific course or project]. I'm now better prepared to take on similar responsibilities."

---

26. Why are you willing to take a pay cut for this job?

Sample Answer:
"While salary is important, my primary focus is on finding a role that aligns with my career goals and provides opportunities for growth. I believe this position offers the chance to contribute meaningfully while expanding my skills and experience."

---

27. How do you respond when your ideas are rejected?

Sample Answer:
"I view rejection as an opportunity to understand other perspectives and refine my approach. For example, when one of my project proposals was turned down, I sought feedback from my manager, reworked the plan, and ultimately gained approval for a revised version."

28. What would your former colleagues say is your biggest flaw?

Sample Answer:
"They might say that I can be overly detail-oriented. While I believe in delivering high-quality work, I've learned to balance this by focusing on deadlines and ensuring the big picture isn't overlooked."

29. If we gave you this job, what would you do in your first 90 days?

Sample Answer:
"In the first 90 days, I would focus on understanding the team's goals and processes, building relationships with colleagues, and identifying areas where I can make immediate contributions. I'd also ensure that I'm fully aligned with your expectations and priorities."

30. Can you give an example of a decision you made that backfired?

Sample Answer:
"In a previous role, I decided to implement a new software tool without involving all stakeholders. While the tool itself was effective, the lack of input from end-users led to resistance. I learned the importance of stakeholder buy-in for successful change management."

31. How do you handle working with someone you don't like?

Sample Answer:
"I focus on maintaining professionalism and finding common ground to achieve shared goals. For example, I once worked with a colleague whose communication style was different from mine. By focusing on the project objectives and being respectful, we were able to collaborate effectively."

32. If you were an animal, what animal would you be and why?

Sample Answer:
"I would be an eagle because it symbolizes focus and vision. Eagles can see the big picture while also zooming in on the details, which reflects my ability to strategize and execute effectively."

33. What's the biggest misconception people have about you?

Sample Answer:
"Some people initially perceive me as reserved because I like to take time to observe and understand situations before speaking. However, once I'm familiar with the team and environment, I'm highly collaborative and communicative."

34. Tell me about a time you disagreed with your boss.

Sample Answer:
"In one case, my manager wanted to pursue a strategy that I believed would be less effective. I respectfully presented data

and alternative options. While the manager ultimately stuck with the original plan, they appreciated my initiative and input."

35. How do you respond to failure?

Sample Answer:
"I view failure as a learning opportunity. For instance, when I missed a critical deadline early in my career, I analyzed what went wrong and implemented a new system to track progress. Since then, I've consistently met deadlines."

36. How do you justify not having more leadership experience at this point in your career?

Sample Answer:
"My focus so far has been on building a strong foundation in my field and becoming an expert in my area. While I've had opportunities to take on informal leadership roles, I'm now actively seeking positions where I can formally lead teams and drive strategic initiatives."

37. Why haven't you achieved more in your career?

Sample Answer:
"While I've achieved a lot that I'm proud of, I believe there's always room for growth. I've taken deliberate steps to develop my skills and experience, but I'm now ready to accelerate my progress in a role that challenges me and offers opportunities for greater impact."

38. If you're so great, why didn't your last employer fight harder to keep you?

Sample Answer:
"My departure wasn't due to a lack of value or contribution but rather a reflection of my desire for growth that the company couldn't accommodate at the time. I left on good terms, and my former manager is one of my biggest advocates, which I'd be happy to demonstrate through a reference."

39. What would you do if you found out your boss was doing something unethical?

Sample Answer:
"I would address the situation professionally and ethically. First, I'd gather the facts to ensure I fully understood the situation. Then, I'd approach my boss privately to discuss my concerns. If the issue wasn't resolved, I'd follow the company's protocol for reporting such matters."

40. If you could eliminate one weakness in your personality, what would it be?

Sample Answer:
"I'd like to be more spontaneous in my approach. While I pride myself on being meticulous and prepared, there are times when thinking on my feet more often could lead to faster decision-making and creative solutions."

41. If you were running this company, what's the first thing you'd change?

Sample Answer:
"It's difficult to assess without being on the inside, but based on my research, I might explore [specific improvement idea based on company's context, e.g., expanding digital marketing efforts or investing in employee training]. That said, I would first listen to employees and stakeholders to ensure I understood their perspectives."

42. Can you describe a situation where you were publicly criticized?

Sample Answer:
"During a team meeting, a manager called out a mistake I'd made in a report. I remained calm, acknowledged the error, and explained how I would correct it. Afterward, I spoke with the manager privately to better understand their concerns. This experience reinforced the importance of thoroughness and proactive communication."

43. How would you handle being assigned a project with almost no direction or guidance?

Sample Answer:
"I would start by clarifying as much as I could with the information available and breaking the project into manageable steps. I'd also proactively reach out to colleagues or stakeholders for additional context if needed. I'm comfortable working independently and taking initiative to ensure success."

44. What would you do if your team consistently underperformed?

Sample Answer:
"I would analyze the root causes—whether it's a lack of clear expectations, resources, or motivation. Then, I'd work with the team to address those issues, set measurable goals, and provide ongoing support. I believe in fostering accountability while empowering my team to succeed."

45. Have you ever made a decision that negatively impacted your team? What did you learn?

Sample Answer:
"Yes, I once prioritized speed over collaboration, which led to misalignment and rework. I realized the importance of involving key stakeholders early on, even if it slows down the initial stages. Since then, I've made collaboration a cornerstone of my approach."

46. What if your manager asked you to do something you strongly disagreed with?

Sample Answer:
"I'd respectfully express my concerns and provide alternative solutions. If the manager insisted, I'd follow through professionally unless it was unethical. In that case, I would escalate the issue following the appropriate company protocols."

47. Why haven't you started your own business if you're this capable?

Sample Answer:
"While I have entrepreneurial ideas, I'm most passionate about contributing to and learning from a team within an established organization. I value the collaboration, resources, and opportunities for impact that come with working in a structured environment."

48. What's the hardest decision you've ever had to make at work?

Sample Answer:
"I once had to recommend cutting a project that my team had worked hard on because it wasn't delivering the expected ROI. It was difficult to deliver that message, but I focused on ensuring the team understood the reasoning and supported them in transitioning to new priorities."

49. How do you deal with underperforming colleagues when their work affects yours?

Sample Answer:
"I address the issue constructively by having a one-on-one conversation to understand their challenges and offer support. If the situation doesn't improve, I escalate the matter to the appropriate manager while continuing to focus on my own responsibilities."

50. Why do you think you've been rejected by other employers?

Sample Answer:
"I've reflected on previous rejections and used them as learning opportunities. In some cases, the roles weren't the best fit for my skills or career goals. I've worked to refine my approach and ensure I'm targeting roles where I can add the most value."

51. Why do you think you deserve this job more than others?

Sample Answer:
"I can't speak for others, but I believe my skills, experience, and passion for [specific field] align perfectly with the role. I'm confident in my ability to deliver results and contribute positively to the team."

52. What's your biggest regret in life?

Sample Answer:
"My biggest regret is not pursuing [specific skill or field] earlier in my career. However, I've worked hard to make up for that by taking courses and gaining hands-on experience."

53. If I spoke to your last boss, what would they say about you?

Sample Answer:
"They'd likely say that I'm dependable, hardworking, and proactive. They might also mention that I'm always looking for ways to improve processes and solve problems."

54. What's the most difficult feedback you've ever received, and how did you handle it?

Sample Answer:
"A manager once told me I needed to improve my presentation skills. I took that feedback seriously, enrolled in a public speaking course, and sought opportunities to present at team meetings. I've since received positive feedback on my presentations."

55. How do you feel about working overtime or on weekends?

Sample Answer:
"I value work-life balance, but I also understand that certain projects may require extra effort. I'm willing to put in additional time when necessary to ensure the team's success."

56. What's the worst mistake you've made at work?

Sample Answer:
"I once sent an email to the wrong client due to a moment of carelessness. I immediately acknowledged the mistake, apologized, and took steps to prevent similar errors, such as double-checking recipient lists."

57. How do you handle favoritism in the workplace?

Sample Answer:
"I focus on staying professional and delivering my best work,

regardless of the situation. If favoritism affects team dynamics or performance, I'd address it respectfully with my manager."

58. What do you think about taking directions from someone younger than you?

Sample Answer:
"Age isn't a factor for me; I respect competence and leadership skills. I'm open to learning from anyone, regardless of their age, as long as it contributes to the team's success."

59. What personal sacrifices are you willing to make for this job?

Sample Answer:
"I'm willing to invest extra time and effort to meet deadlines or complete critical projects. That said, I also believe in maintaining balance to stay productive and motivated in the long term."

60. How would you react if a colleague took credit for your work?

Sample Answer:
"I'd address the situation privately with the colleague to understand their perspective. If the issue persisted, I'd bring it up with my manager to ensure proper recognition."

61. Why do you think your colleagues didn't include you in certain decisions?

Sample Answer:
"Perhaps they felt the decision didn't require my input or believed they had the necessary expertise. I'd use this as an opportunity to improve communication and ensure my contributions are recognized in the future."

---

62. Do you have any health issues that might affect your ability to perform this role?

Sample Answer:
"I'm fully capable of performing all responsibilities required for this role. If any health challenges arise in the future, I'd address them proactively to ensure they don't affect my work."

---

63. What's the most significant personal conflict you've faced at work, and how did you handle it?

Sample Answer:
"I had a disagreement with a colleague over project priorities. I scheduled a one-on-one discussion to understand their perspective and found a compromise that met both our objectives."

---

64. How do you handle it when people criticize you unfairly?

Sample Answer:
"I stay calm and focus on the facts. I address the criticism constructively, providing clarification if necessary, and let my performance speak for itself."

65. Why haven't you achieved a senior-level position yet?

Sample Answer:
"My focus has been on building a strong foundation of skills and experience. I'm now ready to take on senior-level responsibilities and am actively pursuing opportunities like this one."

66. What's the most embarrassing mistake you've made in your career?

Sample Answer:
"Early in my career, I misunderstood a client's requirements and delivered an incomplete report. I immediately took responsibility, corrected the issue, and learned the importance of clarifying expectations upfront."

67. What motivates you to keep working even when things get tough?

Sample Answer:
"My motivation comes from my commitment to delivering quality results and the satisfaction of overcoming challenges. Knowing that my work makes a difference keeps me focused."

68. How do you react when someone questions your competence?

Sample Answer:
"I see it as an opportunity to prove my abilities through my actions. I remain professional and let my work demonstrate my competence."

69. What would you do if you found out your manager was lying to the team?

Sample Answer:
"I'd gather facts and approach the situation delicately. I'd have a private conversation with my manager to understand their perspective and express my concerns about maintaining trust within the team."

70. How do you feel about handling tasks that are not part of your job description?

Sample Answer:
"I'm open to taking on additional tasks that contribute to the team's success. That said, I'd communicate if it became a recurring issue that impacted my core responsibilities."

Here's the continuation with **71 to 101** of the toughest, most challenging, and personal job interview questions, along with suggested answers:

71. Why do you think you haven't been promoted in your previous roles?

Sample Answer:
"In some cases, promotions were tied to tenure rather than merit. While I consistently delivered strong results, the opportunities for advancement were limited. I'm seeking a role where I can grow based on performance and contribution."

72. What would you do if you strongly disagreed with a company policy?

Sample Answer:
"I'd follow the policy while seeking constructive ways to provide feedback through the appropriate channels. My approach would focus on offering solutions rather than just pointing out problems."

---

73. Have you ever had difficulty working with a difficult boss?

Sample Answer:
"Yes, I've worked with a manager whose communication style was very direct, which took some adjustment. I focused on understanding their expectations and adapted my approach to build a stronger working relationship."

---

74. Why do you want to leave your current job so soon?

Sample Answer:
"While I've appreciated my current role, I realized early on that it doesn't align with my long-term career goals. I'm seeking an opportunity that better matches my skills and aspirations."

---

75. What do you fear the most in your career?

Sample Answer:
"My biggest fear is stagnation. I constantly seek opportunities to learn and grow because staying relevant in today's fast-paced world is critical."

76. If we hire you and you fail, what do you think the reason will be?

Sample Answer:
"I believe failure often stems from miscommunication or unclear expectations. I'm committed to maintaining open communication and proactively seeking clarity to ensure I meet or exceed expectations."

77. How do you handle favoritism if it's working against you?

Sample Answer:
"I stay professional and focus on delivering high-quality work. If favoritism affects performance or morale, I'd have a respectful conversation with my manager to address the issue."

78. What would you do if a colleague constantly interrupted you during meetings?

Sample Answer:
"I'd politely address the interruptions during the meeting, asking for the chance to finish my points. If it became a pattern, I'd speak with them privately to resolve the issue."

79. Why are you switching industries at this stage of your career?

Sample Answer:
"I'm seeking a new challenge and believe my transferable skills—like [specific examples]—will add value in this industry. I'm excited about applying my expertise in a different context."

80. What do you think is your greatest professional failure?

Sample Answer:
"I once underestimated the time required for a project, leading to delays. I took responsibility, adjusted the timeline, and implemented better planning techniques for future projects."

81. How do you handle being left out of important decisions at work?

Sample Answer:
"I focus on contributing where I can and proving my value through results. I'd also seek feedback to understand how I could position myself to be included in future discussions."

82. What's a common misconception people have about you?

Sample Answer:
"Some people initially think I'm too serious because I focus intensely on my work. However, once they get to know me, they see that I'm approachable and enjoy collaboration."

83. If you were offered a role at another company tomorrow, what would you do?

Sample Answer:
"I'd evaluate how the role aligns with my career goals, just as I've done with this opportunity. However, I'm genuinely excited about the potential to contribute to your organization."

84. How do you respond to being micromanaged?

Sample Answer:
"I focus on building trust by delivering high-quality work and maintaining open communication. Over time, this usually reduces the need for micromanagement."

85. Have you ever been in a situation where your ethics were challenged?

Sample Answer:
"Yes, I once noticed discrepancies in a report. I brought it to my manager's attention and ensured the issue was resolved transparently and ethically."

86. If you had to fire someone, how would you do it?

Sample Answer:
"I'd ensure the decision was fair and based on objective criteria. I'd deliver the message with empathy, provide clear reasons, and offer support for their transition."

87. Why do you think you were laid off/fired from your last job?

Sample Answer:
"The company underwent restructuring, and my role was impacted. It wasn't a reflection of my performance, as I left on good terms and received positive recommendations."

88. What's your biggest weakness that might affect your ability to succeed here?

Sample Answer:
"I can sometimes be overly detail-oriented, which may slow me down on tight deadlines. However, I've learned to prioritize tasks effectively and focus on the bigger picture."

---

89. What would you do if your boss publicly humiliated you?

Sample Answer:
"I'd remain professional in the moment and address the situation privately later, expressing how it impacted me and seeking to resolve any underlying issues."

---

90. How do you handle being assigned a task outside of your expertise?

Sample Answer:
"I view it as an opportunity to learn and grow. I'd research, consult colleagues, and seek resources to complete the task effectively."

---

91. What if we tell you we don't think you're the best fit for this role?

Sample Answer:
"I'd appreciate the feedback and ask for specific areas where I could improve. I'm always looking to grow and refine my skills."

92. Do you think your previous salary justifies your level of experience?

Sample Answer:
"Salaries often depend on various factors, not just experience. I believe my previous compensation reflected my role at the time, and I'm now seeking a position that aligns with my current skills and contributions."

93. What's one thing your colleagues might find annoying about you?

Sample Answer:
"Some colleagues have found my tendency to ask detailed questions during planning sessions a bit tedious, but it's always helped ensure smooth execution."

94. How do you react to negative performance reviews?

Sample Answer:
"I view them as opportunities to improve. I listen carefully to the feedback, ask for specific examples, and create a plan to address the concerns."

95. What do you do if you feel unappreciated at work?

Sample Answer:
"I focus on delivering results and finding intrinsic motivation in my work. If it becomes a pattern, I'd seek a conversation with my manager to discuss my contributions and ways to improve recognition."

96. Have you ever had a workplace conflict escalate out of control?

Sample Answer:
"Not escalate out of control, but I've had disagreements that required intervention. I always strive to mediate conflicts professionally before they escalate."

---

97. What if we don't offer the growth opportunities you're looking for?

Sample Answer:
"I'd address that by discussing potential paths for growth within the organization. If none were available long-term, I'd still focus on contributing and learning as much as possible."

---

98. Have you ever been accused of something you didn't do at work?

Sample Answer:
"Yes, once I was incorrectly blamed for a missed deadline. I calmly provided evidence to clarify the situation and worked with the team to ensure accountability moving forward."

---

99. How would you handle finding out you were being paid less than your peers?

Sample Answer:
"I'd research market rates and my contributions, then have a respectful conversation with my manager to understand the discrepancy and discuss adjustments."

100. If you're rejected for this role, what will you do next?

Sample Answer:
"I'd be disappointed but would use the feedback to improve and continue pursuing opportunities where I can add value."

101. What's something about you that might make us hesitant to hire you?

Sample Answer:
"Perhaps my lack of direct experience in [specific skill], but I'm confident in my ability to learn quickly and leverage my transferable skills to excel in this role."

www.ingramcontent.com/pod-product-compliance
Lightning Source LLC
Chambersburg PA
CBHW070941220526
45469CB00007B/2471